HIRING YOUR RIGHT #2 LEADER

HIRING YOUR RIGHT #2 LEADER

GAIN MORE TIME
EARN MORE INCOME
CREATE MORE IMPACT

ALEC BROADFOOT

ethos
collective

Printed in the United States of America

Published by Ethos Collective™
PO Box 43, Powell, OH 43065
www.ethoscollective.vip

LCCN: 2024904210
Paperback ISBN: 978-1-63680-259-6
Hardcover ISBN: 978-1-63680-260-2
e-book ISBN: 978-1-63680-261-9

Available in paperback, hardcover, e-book, and audiobook.

Any Internet addresses (websites, blogs, etc.) and telephone numbers printed in this book are offered as a resource. They are not intended in any way to be or imply an endorsement by Ethos Collective™, nor does Ethos Collective™ vouch for the content of these sites and numbers for the life of this book.

EOS® and Strategic Coach® are registered trademarks of their respective companies and their mentions do not represent any endorsement or affiliation with VisionSpark® or the contents of this book.

Some names and identifying details may have been changed to protect the privacy of individuals.

DEDICATION

To my dad - who taught me the importance of hard work, persistence, character and integrity, and to my devoted team members at VisionSpark.

Contents

Foreword

In the ever-evolving landscape of entrepreneurship, where strategic decisions define the trajectory of businesses, Alec Broadfoot's *Hiring Your Right #2 Leader* emerges as a beacon of wisdom and insight. Alec's extensive experience and profound understanding of the delicate dance between leadership and team dynamics make him a trusted guide in the entrepreneurial realm.

I have had the privilege of witnessing countless entrepreneurs navigate the challenges of building and leading successful businesses, and Alec's work stands out as a roadmap for those seeking not just success but sustained growth and fulfillment. *Hiring Your Right #2 Leader* is a call to action, urging entrepreneurs to explore the transformative potential of selecting the ideal second-in-command—be it a Number 2 Leader, Integrator, President, or COO—for their ventures.

In this book, Alec outlines five key takeaways, distilling years of experience into actionable insights that can redefine how entrepreneurs approach team-building and leadership. His emphasis on the game-changing impact of hiring the right second-in-command resonates deeply with my own belief in the power of strategic partnerships within entrepreneurial endeavors.

Alec's dedication to a science-based approach to hiring aligns seamlessly with the principles of Strategic Coach®. By advocating for data-driven decision-making and strategic thinking, Alec challenges entrepreneurs to transcend intuition and embrace a systematic, objective, and forward-thinking perspective in the recruitment process. This alignment is a testament to the effectiveness of Alec's approach and its resonance with proven methodologies for entrepreneurial success.

Furthermore, Alec's exploration of search firms, recruiters, and the nuances of the hiring process reflects a comprehensive understanding of the challenges entrepreneurs face. His insights empower entrepreneurs to navigate this complex terrain with confidence, aligning with the commitment to continuous learning and growth that is at the core of the Strategic Coach® philosophy.

What sets Alec apart is his embodiment of the "Who Not How" concept that we teach at Strategic Coach®. In the spirit of this powerful idea, Alec is not merely a guide on hiring; he is a "who" finder. His expertise in identifying the right individuals to propel your business forward aligns seamlessly with the essence of "Who Not How." In Alec's approach, he doesn't just tell you how to hire a Number 2 Leader; he shows you who can make it happen.

As you delve into the pages of *Hiring Your Right #2 Leader*, I encourage you to embrace Alec's wisdom as a valuable asset in your entrepreneurial journey. Alec's focus on avoiding common hiring mistakes and the transformative role of business coaching, particularly with an EOS Implementer, aligns perfectly with the ethos of Strategic Coach®—an organization dedicated to empowering entrepreneurs to reach their full potential.

May this book be the catalyst for a new era of strategic hiring, where entrepreneurs, inspired by Alec's guidance, build teams that not only drive business success but also enhance personal joy and fulfillment.

Here's to Alec Broadfoot, whose work is shaping the future of entrepreneurship, and to all entrepreneurs who will undoubtedly find immense value and inspiration within the pages of *Hiring Your Right #2 Leader*.

Dan Sullivan

Co-Founder & President, Strategic Coach®

66

WHO NOT HOW.

———————————

Dan Sullivan

Introduction

Have you ever heard this quote - "An entrepreneur is someone who is willing to work eighty hours a week so they can avoid working forty hours?"

Most people would shake their heads hearing this quote, thinking this is the definition of craziness. The rest of us, the entrepreneurs among us, smile and nod. We wear a crazy number of hats, achieve more in a day than many achieve in a month, and we're thinking about our business 24/7. There is no off button.

But with this tremendous creative energy, productivity, and drive also typically comes a blind spot, as was certainly true in my case. I call this blind spot the "hiring chasm." As entrepreneurs, we're used to moving fast and making important decisions on the fly. That includes hiring decisions. We think that we can make good hiring decisions based on our gut.

It turns out we can't. No one can, really.

What's amazing is that sometimes we can have decent success even with bad hires. **Where the wheels come off, though, is when we want to grow.** There is no way you can truly take your company where you want to go unless you make the right hires, recruiting people who fit your culture and have what it takes to go into the unknown and grow with you.

This book has one goal: to help entrepreneurs like you hire the right Number 2 leader. To do that, I need to pull the curtain back on my world for you.

My company, VisionSpark, has had uncommon success when it comes to finding the right leaders for entrepreneurial companies. In fact, we made the 2023 Inc. 5000 list as one of the fastest growing companies in the United States.

I have seen all the mistakes—and have made a healthy percentage of them myself. This means you won't have to. If I am successful in what I will be illustrating for you in these pages, then you will develop the kind of vision you need to fill in your hiring blind spot and take a significant leap forward in scaling your business and meeting and exceeding your growth goals.

That journey, I argue, begins with hiring the right Number 2 Leader. The exact title for your Number 2 leader may vary depending on the nature of your business. Some options I hear a lot include COO, President, Integrator™, Second in Command (2iC), Conductor, Orchestrator, General Manager, Chief of Staff, Operator. The title and position may vary based on the industry.

On the following pages I'm going to share some of our most valuable hiring practices at VisionSpark and give you the kind of help and roadmap that I wish I'd had when I was hiring my first Number 2 Leader.

We will start with some of my story. I think you'll find it helpful to understand a bit of my own entrepreneurial background, as well as to hear about my worst ever hire that turned things around for me and my former company. From there, we will look at what having the right COO—the right Number 2 Leader—will do for your business and for you personally. We will also identify the key success attributes your Number 2 needs to have, the biggest hiring mistakes you will want to avoid, and much more.

I would also like to offer my personal help. If at any point you need clarification or wish to discuss your situation, please reach out to me at Alec@Vision-Spark.com. As entrepreneurs, we belong to a special club together, and I would love to help you do what you do even better.

66

I WAKE UP EVERY MORNING
AND THINK TO MYSELF,
'HOW FAR CAN
I PUSH THIS COMPANY IN
THE NEXT 24 HOURS?'

———————

Leah Busque

CHAPTER ONE

Harnessing Your Entrepreneurial Superpower

I sometimes joke that I was an accidental entrepreneur, but that is only partly true. The greater truth is that I knew in my heart that I wanted to be in business for myself, I just expected that it would come much later in life. When I was "ready."

Now I know, as you no doubt do, that being an entrepreneur is just who you are. You can't prepare for it. But you can make the most of it. There are methods and approaches and strategies that will help guide you on this entrepreneurial journey.

That is my goal here. To guide you in hiring your COO, your Number 2 Leader, and maybe even persuading you that this is something you *should really do* if you're still on the fence about it. I want you to make the most of your entrepreneurial superpower, and this can only happen with the right people in the right seats. This book is all about what that means and how you can make it happen for yourself and your company.

The Accidental Entrepreneur

My journey as an entrepreneur began when I was twenty-five and was presented with the opportunity to buy a small publishing business with some friends. We were on vacation together, and I was fresh out of school with my MBA. They were asking me a lot of questions because they wanted to buy the mom-and-pop business they were working for. The business published a reference guide for the collectibles industry and sold about 30,000 copies a year, with two yearly updates. This was old-school mail order, with an 800 number and a mailing list. There was no website because all this was in the incredibly early days of the internet. At one point, they turned to me and said, "We should buy this together."

I couldn't say no.

The reason I couldn't say no was because I already knew that I wanted to be in business for myself, even though it initially went against the advice of my father and the focus of my MBA schooling, which was to prepare us to be CEOs of big companies.

My father, one of my biggest role-models, taught me early on the importance of persistence and never giving up—a critical attribute for any entrepreneur. He always had my best interests at heart and had given me what may have been good advice for most people at that time: get a college degree, work for a good company, and they'll take care of you. But I couldn't follow that advice because in my heart I knew I was an entrepreneur. A tiger can't change his stripes.

So, I became a business owner at age twenty-five. To be honest, I then spent the next ten years making all the worst hiring decisions of my life—not only with the publishing business that I bought with my friends—that business soon went online and had a good run. But my next business was a mailing company that also did some light printing. We processed mail for all the large corporations in our city and had a printing operation that ran two shifts—about 30–35 employees overall.

This company was where I first had to deal with hiring in a tangible way, and it was trial by fire. I am almost embarrassed to say that seven out of ten employees either quit or were fired. I'm a good judge of character, but we had serious retention issues. For a long time, I blamed it on the talent pool or economic conditions. It was something else. It was *me*, and I soon had all the evidence I needed for that conclusion.

My Worst Hire Teaches Me a Lesson

They really don't teach you how to hire properly in school. Even in HR programs, you aren't really taught how to interview effectively. Most people do what I was doing—interview the best candidates I could find and then hire mostly on how you feel about them.

At one point, however, I figured that there had to be a better way, so I reached out to one of my mentors for guidance. Among other things, he recommended a hiring assessment tool for learning about an individual's personality and their mental aptitude so that we could quickly qualify or disqualify them for the job. That such a strategy even existed was a revelation to me, and I was all for using it.

And we did use it—sort of.

The main reason I finally contacted my mentor was that we had been having a tough time hiring an office assistant. We had gone through at least four assistants over a year, and it was a crucial role. In hindsight, I clearly see that despite my MBA and good character instincts, I didn't know what I was doing. I didn't really know how to write a job description, for instance, and matching someone to our work culture was not even an afterthought.

We tried everything, including upping the salary for the office assistant, but we just couldn't find anyone qualified who was also willing to do the job. But then we interviewed a lovely woman, and she knocked the interview out of the park. I really thought we had finally found our assistant. Although I didn't think it was even necessary, we also had her take the assessment tool that my mentor had recommended.

In aviation, to become a pilot you need to do what is called instrument training, which is flying solely using your instruments. The reason for this is that, especially in harsh weather, things can get dangerously uncertain if you are relying on your senses. The same is pretty much true for hiring, as I soon learned the hard way.

To my surprise, the assessment tool results for the woman I wanted to hire were horrible. It said she was going to be a super slow learner and have low attention to detail. It also said she would be a social butterfly, procrastinate, and need a lot of hand holding and affirmation.

My gut told me that the assessment had gotten her wrong. Just to make sure, I checked her references. They all said, "Oh, she's great. We enjoyed speaking with her." Feeling vindicated, I hired her. As you've probably guessed, it was a big mistake. Everything in the assessment turned out to be true—social butterfly, low attention to detail, very insecure. It was a complete disaster, and we fired her after only three weeks.

People Problems, Not Cash Flow Problems

Fast forward a couple of years. Not long after learning this life-changing lesson from my worst hire, I sold my share in the mailing and printing company. Long story short, we reversed our hiring problem and now seven out of ten employees stayed with us. Things were great.

But the truth was that my heart was no longer in that business. I wanted to be involved in something where I could have more opportunities for growth and where I could help other business owners. I had already started doing some consulting for companies struggling with cash flow and profitability, so selling my share in the company meant that I was now freed up to do even more of this kind of work.

I was excited again. I really enjoyed helping other businesses optimize their operations. It felt like my calling. Soon, however, I realized that many businesses did not have a cash flow problem—*they had a people problem.*

I remember one business, for example, a landscaping business with two partners. I was hired to help them get out of debt and deal with the IRS, and we were making great progress increasing their margins and profitability. We were able to uncover a real problem: one of the partners had a sister who worked in the office, and it was a bad fit. To be blunt, it was toxic, and it was causing a huge rift between the partners. It got so bad that one of the partners hated going to work.

This was not the only place I saw such problems. I often saw situations where the wrong employees were the leaders, or key personnel were not up to the job for one reason or another. All of this was affecting morale and profitability at these companies. The bottom line was that they did not really have a profitability problem; they had hired or promoted the wrong people. The disconnect was something that I could not only see, but that I also knew how to fix.

The Blind Spot

There are few things more costly to a company than a bad hire, and in my experience, this is especially true for entrepreneurial companies. Yet most entrepreneurs have a blind spot when it comes to hiring. They usually base their hiring decisions on their heart and their gut, as I had done unsuccessfully, *and they don't use data*. This means that they have trouble making objective hiring decisions.

This brings us back to you and your company.

Hiring your Number 2 Leader, your COO, will be the most significant hire in the history of your business. Not only do I want you to get it right, but I want to *help* you get it right. For that, we will need to leave my story behind and focus for the rest of this book on how you can hire your Number 2, which will allow you to harness your entrepreneurial superpower and really take off.

As you already know, the culture of an entrepreneurial company is rather intimate, so you can't have the same hiring process as a big corporation.

Your company is like a family in many ways, which means you're looking for a particular person. Someone that matches *you* and the entrepreneurial growth culture you've created.

It's vitally important to hire a Number 2 who's a cultural and team fit, has great character values, and complements the entrepreneur or entrepreneurs who founded the company.

I like to say that the Number 2 Leader must be the Yin to the Visionary's Yang.

Let's get into it.

66

WHEN YOUR WORK FITS YOUR GIFTS AND YOUR ABILITIES, YOUR WHOLE WORLD BECOMES BRIGHTER.

———————————

Dave Wilbert

CHAPTER TWO

Why Hiring Your Number 2 Leader Will Be a Business Game Changer

A s an entrepreneur, *who are you?*

I ask this question because you really need to think about it. You need to understand what you are bringing to your entrepreneurial venture.

What, in other words, are you doing that no one else can do?

You may be wearing many hats, and perhaps doing so extremely well, but doing everything is simply not efficient. For one, many things you've assumed responsibility for are diluting what you do best. You don't have the time and energy to focus on your business as a whole.

You have probably heard the maxim that you can't work *in* your business and *on* your business at the same time.

Here's another angle: How many entrepreneurs does it take to change a light bulb? One, but the bulb never gets changed because an entrepreneur will happily take on the challenge of working in the dark. In other words, some of the very qualities that make you an entrepreneur to begin with can also be counterproductive when misapplied.

Of course, I get it that in the beginning you may have to do most everything, and a big part of that is that you see how it all fits together, how everything must work. That is because you are the Visionary. As an entrepreneur, you are the venture's Visionary, and no one else can see things like you do.

The other side of this is that you are doing many things that are outside the scope of your expertise and superpower.

There are many challenges that you probably don't enjoy, such as employee issues, running meetings, holding people accountable, or executing a business plan. You are responsible for solving every problem, whether you're strong in that area or not. You are also traveling a lot of distances in your brain and making sharp turns as you talk finance with your bookkeeper, then you're suddenly in a sales and marketing meeting, followed immediately by an operations meeting. It's mentally exhausting as well as inefficient.

As the Visionary, you are number one. The leader of everything. I would like you to understand that, as impressive as this is, it's also extremely limiting.

When you hire your Number 2, *your world changes.* You can do what is actually best for your business, which is to work *on* the business as opposed to *in* the business.

You can do the things that you do best and enjoy the most. When you are not in the weeds of the business's everyday challenges, you can focus on new sales, new services, your business's big relationships, and technology to improve operations because you have been freed up. You're not running around putting out fires or getting involved in decisions that someone else could manage just as well (or probably better, because that is what they enjoy). Your business will be able to scale; you could have ten times growth, rather than 10 percent growth.

One of the biggest challenges I see obstructing entrepreneurs is a simple mindset problem. Entrepreneurs are ready to do what it takes, and this often translates into "everything is supposed to be difficult, and you just have to work hard." The reality is that you can actually hire someone who loves solving problems and overcoming obstacles. It may be strange for you to imagine that people genuinely like doing those things that you don't really or don't really need to do. Dan Sullivan of the Strategic Coach ® program is famous for saying, "Who Not How."

Value: The Game-Changing Mindset Shift

The shift in mindset that will free you and your business comes down to *value*. What you are good at is what is most valuable to your business and that needs to sink in.

Value is a multiplier. This means that concentrating on the value that you bring to the venture will increase the value of the business as well as your personal sense of satisfaction and achievement. **If you are doing fifteen-dollar-an-hour work, then that means that you are withholding value from the business** (in the next chapter, we will do an exercise to demonstrate what your time is truly worth).

Bottom line: the value you add to your business by being the Visionary doing the high-level strategic and big-picture work creates efficiency and opportunity far beyond anything that can be done on the level of everyday tasks and minor problem-solving.

The measure of this added value turns out to be your energy, your passion. What I see repeatedly—and what happened to me—is that once you have freed yourself to do only what brings the most value to your business, the things you enjoy and are good at, then you have more energy and more passion. **You may fall in love with your business again.**

There are so many clients we've worked with that had thoughts of closing their business down because they didn't want to deal with the problems anymore, the customer issues, employee issues. **Once they hired that Number 2 Leader, they no longer had those thoughts anymore, and their business took off.**

The Right People in the Right Seats

How does this happen? Having a Number 2 Leader means having more time on your hands. So, you'll be working on the things you're good at, and you will also have the freedom to spend time with your family and take vacations. More free days equal more freedom. This means more joy and more creative, expansive visionary thinking. Things that were not even possible to think about when you were stressed and overstretched now become intriguing problems to consider and find creative solutions to.

Let's take this one step further. *You should also consider how this increased energy and freedom may add to your business's valuation.*

For example, you have now been freed up by hiring a Number 2 Leader. With your new time, you can bring in a big client that will bring seven figures in increased sales to your business. Assuming your business has a 30% profit margin, and your business is valued at a multiple of 7 times EBITDA, the profit from your new million-dollar client will increase the enterprise value of the business by *over two million dollars.*

$1m client x 30% profit margin =
$300,000 profit from new client
7 (current multiple) x $300,000 (new profit) =
$2.1m (increase in your enterprise value)

Remember how I told you earlier that businesses mostly have a people problem, not a cash flow problem? **With a second in command, there is someone to do everything not suited to your superpowers.** Your Number 2 has complementary skills to yours. Maybe they're more objective and are strong where you are not as strong. They also have strong business and financial acumen.

What will this mean? Together, you will be a force multiplier. And this means that their salary will not be an issue. Sometimes people will say to me, "Alec, I'd love to hire a Number 2, but I can't afford someone at that level." **The reality is that your Number 2 Leader will deliver multiple times what you pay them in actual value to your business.** They're going to pay for their salary by being financially astute, making great business decisions, and by giving you the ability to focus on your top line and generate revenue.

Of course, this means you've hired the right person. So, let's talk next about what your Number 2 Leader's key success attributes need to be.

66

CULTURE EATS STRATEGY
FOR BREAKFAST.

———————————

Peter Drucker

CHAPTER THREE

The Key Success Attributes Your Number 2 Leader Must Have

Your Number 2 has a rare combination of talents and qualities, but that does not make hiring the right Number 2 a rare event. At VisionSpark, we routinely help entrepreneurs do exactly that—successfully hire the right Number 2 Leader. Our secret? We know what we are looking for, and we know how to recognize it when we see it. I'm going to share much of that with you in this chapter.

As we clarified earlier, your Number 2 must complement your skills, *not replicate them*. You are not trying to hire your clone. Quite the opposite. This means that you need to be clear about who you are, what you are good at, and what you enjoy, so that you hire the right Number 2 who fits harmoniously. Like a good co-pilot, your Number 2 knows and understands the direction your company is heading, but your Number 2 takes care of things that free you up. In fact, your Number 2 *protects* your freedom so that you can accomplish more of what you do best.

Some examples include:

1. Steve Jobs and Steve Wozniak (Apple):

- ○ Steve Jobs was the visionary and charismatic leader.

- ○ Steve Wozniak was the technical genius responsible for designing the Apple I and II computers.

2. Bill Gates and Paul Allen (Microsoft):

- ○ Bill Gates was the strategic thinker and business mind.

- ○ Paul Allen was the programming and technical talent who co-founded Microsoft.

3. Sherlock Holmes and Dr. John Watson (Literature):

- ○ Sherlock Holmes, the brilliant and eccentric detective.

- ○ Dr. John Watson, his loyal and practical friend, chronicled their adventures.

4. Batman and Robin (Comics):

- ○ Batman, the brooding and resourceful detective.

- ○ Robin, the youthful and agile sidekick.

5. **Simon and Garfunkel (Music):**

- Paul Simon was the songwriter and guitarist.

- Art Garfunkel was the vocalist with a distinctive voice.

We have already discussed the vital importance of valuing your time and your Visionary responsibilities, but we need to revisit this for a moment from a slightly different angle because it will bring home the understanding about why having a Number 2 is essential for the success of your business. **Your responsibility as the entrepreneur, as the Visionary entrepreneur, is to spend your time on revenue-generating activities.** This is virtually impossible when you are tied to the daily operations and decisions of your business. To keep with the aviation metaphors, you can't properly chart your best course if you never reach cruising altitude.

A powerful exercise that every entrepreneur should undertake is to make a record of everything you do, every activity you complete and every decision that you make, over the course of a full week. Then tally all the time you spent on genuine revenue-generating activities.

The results will probably shock you.

One study I read reported that purely revenue-generating activities accounted for fewer than two hours per day, and sometimes much less. But let's not stop there. You can use your numbers to see the actual hourly rate that your time is worth. To do this, first take the number of hours you recorded of actual revenue-generating activities that you recorded during that week, and now multiply it by fifty-two to represent a year. Next, take your annual salary and divide it by the number of hours you just calculated for the year.

Let's take those two productive hours per day figure, and say that, like most entrepreneurs, we work six days per week for fifty weeks per year. That is 600 hours per year, and if we make $300,000 per year, that means that our time is worth $500 per hour! That number is a general approximation of what your time is worth, and it's also a number you should keep in mind the next time you are doing something far below your pay grade.

And we are not done with this exercise yet.

It's a safe bet that your current salary or take-home pay is not the salary you want. You have a different number in your head for what you would like to be making, so now take that number and divide it by the number of hours you calculated for a full year of your revenue-generating activity. And please note that these activities you count toward your weekly total are the time spent doing actual revenue- generating activities. Conversations and learning or studying do not count, unless it was a sales conversation that led to an actual sale or piece of revenue-generating business.

If we simply doubled the number we used earlier to $600,000 per year, that would mean that our new per-hour value is $1,000 per hour! This new number, calculated from your desired income, can be viewed as the actual per-hour value of your time because you will never achieve your goal if you do not begin to see it and believe it. If you don't act like your time is worth $1,000 per hour, it probably never will be.

The point of this exercise, however, is not just to show you how you are wasting your time. The point is to really drive home the need for a Number 2 Leader to give more opportunity for you to do your real work as a Visionary entrepreneur. It should also stress the importance of a clearly defined and executed strategy—which brings us to your Number 2.

Strategic Thinking and Mental Aptitude

One of the most important things we test in our evaluations of prospective Number 2s is mental acuity. You need to have a good sense of your Number 2 Leader's capacity for learning, reasoning, making good judgments, and problem solving. Your Number 2 Leader needs to be a strategic thinker, which involves mental acuity and their tendency to being strong in organization. And by organized, I do not mean that they keep their office tidy. I am talking about true organization, which means the ability to prioritize, anticipate, predict, plan, and manage time well.

Strategic thinking is actually a suite of skills and aptitudes that are informed by, you guessed it, vision.

A strategic thinker is not necessarily a Visionary, but someone who plans and *executes from a vision*. In the case of your Number 2, strategic thinking must also include being process oriented. They need to be able to come up with processes and see them through implementation. This is different from being options-oriented, which is usually more how entrepreneurs operate.

One way I have seen successful Number 2 Leaders work is by knowing how to systematically question the suggestions and ideas the entrepreneur comes up with. Sometimes the Visionary entrepreneur can get caught up in the appeal of a new idea, in line with the options-oriented framework. A strategic Number 2 Leader knows how to sort through the soundness of the idea to decide if it fits into the business strategy. This is done through knowledge-based questioning and open-mindedness. Your Number 2 Leader will never be disrespectful of your ideas, but you also count on them to assess their real value and potential. They are patient, tactful, and objective.

A Number 2 can be this way because they are, at heart, people-oriented and not task-oriented. This is another vital quality of your Number 2. They love to lead, inspire, and coach people. And to do this well, a successful Number 2 will need to systemize operations. This is essential for the execution of a coherent strategy.

Playbooks and Accountability

The implementation of strategy requires what used to be called standard operating procedures. Nowadays people speak of playbooks, which are systematized strategies that have been formatted into a process. A playbook is a better term because it reflects that there are decision points that allow for flexibility. A playbook can also incorporate new learning so that the playbook is being regularly updated to reflect the most current knowledge. For example, there will be a playbook for client acquisition or for service updates.

One of the important aspects of playbooks is that they create accountability. Roles, procedures, and responsibilities are clearly documented, and your Number 2 Leader is the one who is responsible not only for creating or improving these playbooks but also for holding people in the company accountable. This is another reason your Number 2 Leader must also be a strong communicator. They love to communicate and include all the necessary details for the sake of clarity and accountability. And since they love to manage and coach people, they see ensuring accountability as a natural extension of the effective implementation of strategy. Holding people accountable with measurables is not conflict; it should be seen as part of creating and supporting a strong culture where all can learn, grow, and succeed.

At this point, you can see that **a successful Number 2 Leader is good at overcoming obstacles, solving problems, protecting the Visionary's time, communicating, strategic thinking, and implementation.** This is an exceedingly rare skill set held by less than 3 percent of the population. It's not a large segment of the workforce, in other words. They are also often underutilized or overlooked because their ideal role is so misunderstood.

I should also mention that the salary for a Number 2 Leader will vary greatly by industry, company size, geography, and experience, so it is not possible to give you an estimate.

If you want to know about your specific situation, you can call us, and we will give you an estimate for your situation.

Next up we need to talk about how you can attract and find your Number 2 Leader.

66

HIRING IS A DISCOVERY PROCESS.

Bob Spence

Chapter Four

Beyond the Job Description

Why "JDs" are Hopelessly Outdated and Why You Need a Science-Based Approach Instead

The vast majority of job descriptions are almost comically wrong for hiring the kind of talent you need for an entrepreneurial company. Think about it. They are mostly written in a neutral, anonymous tone, and they just highlight what they want from an applicant. They are so neutral, in fact, that you could pretty much just swap out the hiring company's name for any other.

These standard job descriptions also usually list about twenty-five responsibilities, and it sounds like you're going to be tucked away in some cubicle somewhere grinding out your day. The only real selling point in such a job description is the salary, so it had better be extremely generous if you wish to get any responses at all from top-tier talent. Chances are, though, that the best candidates won't even send in a resume.

Your company has a very distinct culture—as do all entrepreneurial companies. You want to promote and advertise that culture because top talent wants to work for great organizations *because* of the culture. Standard job descriptions won't cut it, and they are so hopelessly outdated that any mention of culture or working environment is only an afterthought or just a list of boilerplate attitudes. All of that is meaningless and doesn't communicate any priorities. In fact, what it is basically saying is, "Hey, we don't care about you as a person. We only care about you getting all this done."

Position Profiles

What works instead is to use a science-based approach that magnetically draws in the kind of people you want to hire. At VisionSpark, we don't even call them job descriptions; we call them position profiles. A properly done position profile will completely flip the script on the hiring conversation.

Instead of you trying to sell the company to the candidate, *the candidates are trying to sell themselves to the company.* My team gets to hear things every day from candidates like "I read your posting, and this is me. I want to work for this company!"

The reason position profiles work so well is the candidates will see themselves in the profile and *feel the synergy.*

The science component is present in that the candidates are subliminally taking themselves through our evaluation steps. The position profile reflects the company's core values, culture, and how it measures and values success. I see it as a qualitative blueprint of the person you want to hire, so when the right person reads, they feel compelled to respond because they can see and feel themselves in this role.

The position profile will not only attract those who align with the values and skills needed to succeed in this role and culture, but the profile will also automatically sort out those who are not a fit. They will just not be interested because there is no resonance, and they don't want to waste their time. This sorting process is important because it means you will not be doing a lot of pointless interviews.

The position profile is of course only one part of our search process—at the end of this chapter, I will share an outline of our process with you, so that you can see the steps involved. I will share some of that process now because you need to understand how you can attract and hire your Number 2 Leader.

A Science-Based Search Approach

As you may have guessed, putting together an effective position profile takes a great deal of strategic thinking, as well as an in-depth understanding of your company culture. Our process begins with meeting with the Visionary so that we understand who they are looking for and what kind of person will work with them. We ask a lot of questions, and we also incorporate the Visionary's behavior and personality.

From there, we meet with those who we call the stakeholders in this hiring. Typically, this will be the key team members. We ask the key team members about what they believe should be the attributes of their future Number 2 Leader. In this way, we are getting buy-in from them; rather than the hire being seen as the Visionary's pick, they now feel that they have a voice in the hire also. You could even say that after interviewing the Visionary about the hire, we then interview the key team members. Nearly 100 percent of the time, the Visionary and the key team members say the same thing, but we are seeing it from the other side of the equation. If there is any significant discrepancy, we can explore that to find resolution.

Having this depth of input is what allows you to write a compelling position profile.

The process can be complex, but that is what is needed to pinpoint what should go in the position profile as well as how the interviewing should go. Our interviewing process has two levels. The first interview is a screening interview in which we evaluate their credentials, management and leadership experience. We also conduct an eight-question, research-based management interview. The second interview is a thorough leadership study that evaluates each candidate in 12 essential leadership capabilities.

I believe it would be useful and instructive for you to understand a little more deeply how we conduct the candidate interviews.

Our interview questions are based on psychological and linguistic research that allow us to understand what the "right" answers are. If the candidate doesn't give enough of the right answers, then they get eliminated.

Let me give you an example of a question we use so that you can understand better how this works. We might start by saying, "A manager achieves many things. What accomplishments give you the greatest satisfaction?" This is a carefully worded and selected question, and we know exactly what we are looking for.

Answers that we get may be something like: "I started an operation in Raleigh, and we grew that branch from ten employees to thirty employees" or "My greatest accomplishment is that there was a plant in Saint Louis that was underperforming, and I turned it around, so it became cash flow positive."

These are the wrong answers.

The right answer is: "my greatest accomplishment is building teams, seeing other people succeed."

If a candidate scores strongly in each of the areas in this study, they are moved on to the next level of the interview process.

You can see from this information that it is possible to evaluate candidates scientifically. We also have all our top candidates complete an online assessment called the Talent Impact Profile™ (talentimpactprofile.com), which evaluates *six mental aptitudes* including mental acuity, which we discussed earlier. This assessment measures strategic and critical thinking, problem-solving, attention to detail, ability to work with numbers, understanding of business terms, and vocabulary. The assessment also measures personality, behaviors, and tendencies, and helps us determine if they fit with the given success pattern for that role.

As you can see, we do heavy vetting of the candidates. The stakes are high. A bad hire will not only be financially expensive, but it will also have a lasting impact on morale and other intangibles of your company culture.

Hopefully, you are beginning to understand that as important as it is for the growth and success of your business to hire a Number 2 Leader, it is equally important to put the right people in the right seats. In our next section, we will look at what it takes to do all this in-house and compare it to engaging a search firm.

66

THE BEST TIME TO FIRE A POOR PERFORMER IS DURING THE INTERVIEW PROCESS.

———————————

Fred Crum

CHAPTER FIVE

How to Find Your Number 2 Leader

SHOULD YOU DIY OR USE A SPECIALIST?

A s we just covered, we have discovered at VisionSpark that we get the best results with a science-based approach. From crafting the position profile and consulting key team members for buy-in to interviewing the candidate, we rely on behavioral science, including linguistics and research on leadership, to ensure that we find and hire the right Number 2 for our entrepreneur clients.

This is not to say that you can't do the hiring yourself. You can, and what I cover in this section should help you a lot if that is the way you are going. **You need to be prepared, however, to spend the time needed to make a successful hire.** Being methodical is the only way to get this right, and you need to set aside at least 200 hours. Getting it wrong will not only set you back a pretty penny, which we will go over in a moment, but it will also cost you, according to Brad Smart, another 278 hours in addition to the 200 hours necessary for the hiring process.

Gallup tells us that 82 percent of the time, companies fail to hire the right manager. In other words, the average employer has only an **18 percent success rate** in hiring leaders!

This figure matches my own informal survey, where I ask visionaries to tell me how many of their last ten hires they would rehire, knowing what they know now.

The standard answer is two or three, which is in the ballpark of the Gallup figure.

The reason I believe that this number is so low is that we are talking about complex operations that involve complex, sensitive human beings. Add to that all the misinformation and incomplete information we have about human motivations and human relationships, and maybe that 18% number is damn good for shooting from the hip.

But however we slice it, the odds are not in your favor.

You need to sort out the pretenders from the contenders, how to create a position profile, and where to get the right people to read it. You also need to interview extremely well and use assessment tools to reveal what is subconscious and hidden. And then there is also the science of crafting an offer, potentially the need to negotiate salary, and onboarding.

The downside of a mis-hire is not fun. In addition to the hours the hiring process consumed, and the hours taken up sorting out that a mistake was made, there are tangible and intangible costs that add up quickly. The standard rule of thumb is that getting it wrong will cost at least three times their annual salary, and I have even seen assessments that put the financial cost much higher—as much as fourteen times annual salary. Ouch. That's a big hit to absorb.

There are also the intangible "soft costs" of company and customer morale, not to mention your own frustrations and disappointments. I have even seen companies eventually fold in the aftermath of an unfortunate leadership hire.

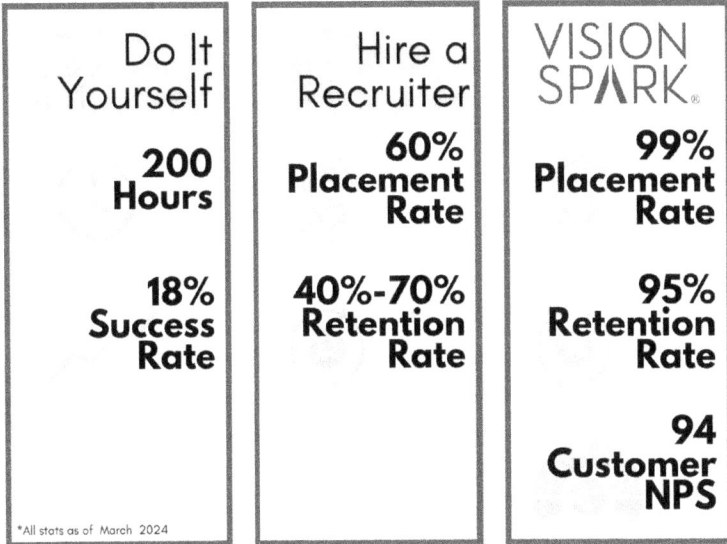

Do It Yourself	Hire a Recruiter	VISION SPARK®
200 Hours	**60% Placement Rate**	**99% Placement Rate**
18% Success Rate	**40%-70% Retention Rate**	**95% Retention Rate**
*All stats as of March 2024		**94 Customer NPS**

Alternatives to DIY

Of course, the complexities and potential risks around hiring are precisely why so many companies choose to hire specialists, just as they hire outside accounting firms and employment law firms. An outside perspective can also help you see potential problems and identify valuable assets or circumstances that you may not otherwise see. Self-evaluations are notoriously incomplete because we tend not to notice what has become commonplace or built into the fabric of our culture.

Recruiters vs. Search Firms

The alternatives to doing it yourself are perhaps also understandably complex, and entrepreneurial companies especially need to understand the players and details of the hiring industry.

To start with, let me take a moment here to clarify the differences between recruiters and executive search firms (like Vision-Spark). While there are some good recruiters out there, especially in specialty areas such as computer programming languages or highway paving engineers, the recruiting business is a transaction-based business with a low success rate—much less than 50 percent. They guarantee their hires for three to six months, and in exchange they take a percentage of the yearly salary as payment. They do little evaluation of the person's job credentials and truly little interviewing. They generally don't take a company's culture into account, either, which is why they are especially not suitable for entrepreneurial companies.

With a search firm, on the other hand, you are dealing with a senior level person who is an experienced search consultant, who is trained to provide a much more rigorous evaluation of the candidate, including strong interviewing—such as the strategic interviewing we do. Search firms focus on culture and core values, and they work by exclusive arrangement. This means that you are committed to using them, and they are committed to finding that person for you. The industry average placement rate among search firms is around 60 percent. VisionSpark, I am proud to say, has a 98 percent success rate.

Key Differentiators

When engaging a specialist to do your hiring, such as a specialty search firm like VisionSpark, you need to understand what differentiates one from the next.

Do they have a focus, such as an industry or a position (CEO, COO, etc.), or a niche focus (like VisionSpark and entrepreneurs)?

Remember, you are basically hiring them to find your Number 2, the most important hiring decision you will make.

Flat Fee (VisionSpark) or Hourly or Salary Percentage?

One extremely important differentiator is the price of service. Nearly all search firms, for example, will charge you a percentage of the position's salary. The higher the first-year compensation, the more you will pay this firm. This is standard practice in the industry. However, at VisionSpark, we charge a flat fee, so you can be certain that any recommendations we make for your new hire are not linked to our compensation. We have other reasons for this policy, but you will find that we are unique in this regard.

Hire Guarantee

Search companies also have varying policies on how long they will keep the search open and how long they guarantee that the hired candidate will stay. For many firms, the hire guarantee ranges between six and nine months, but at VisionSpark we guarantee that we will find this person and won't stop until you tell us. Further, our all-star guarantee is that they'll be there for a year, so, if they resign or get fired, we'll redo the process for no charge. As far as I know, VisionSpark is the first in the industry to offer both of these guarantees.

Onboarding

You also need to be clear on how the search firm pulls together the right salary offer for you, as well as what their onboarding process will be like. The onboarding piece is especially important, for we find that the better the onboarding process, the better you have effective integration of the new hire, your Number 2. Of course, onboarding also goes better if you have gotten buy-in from the key team members and stakeholders early in the process, as we have already discussed.

Just to give you something to compare to, our onboarding process has four separate phases: the initial onboarding, a thirty-day check-in, a ninety-day check-in, and a 180-day check-in.

At each of those check-in points we perform comparative assessments for the Visionary and the Number 2, detailing where things are strong and where there is an opportunity for greater collaboration and strategic synergy.

I also need to emphasize how important the first onboarding weeks are. **You need to spend real, substantial time with the new hire, with orientation, and let them know in concrete terms how they're going to be held accountable and how their performance is going to be measured.** They need to be clear about what success looks like within the first few days of employment. It's not like you can just hand them the keys, say welcome aboard and tell them to holler if they need anything.

The bottom line, whether you try and do it yourself or hire a specialist, comes down to opportunity costs and what your time is worth. Being in the weeds while you're trying to hire someone generally prevents you from focusing on what you do best as a Visionary and what's best for your company.

As you see, there are quite a few advantages to engaging a search firm to help you hire and onboard your Number 2, so in the next section we will go over specific questions to ask the specialists so that you can go with the one that is best for you.

66

GREAT VISION WITHOUT GREAT PEOPLE IS IRRELEVANT.

———————

Jim Collins

CHAPTER SIX

All Search Firms Are Not Created Equal

UNDERSTANDING THE DIFFERENCES AND KNOWING WHAT QUESTIONS TO ASK

W e have already covered a fair amount of information about the differences among search firms, as well as the difference between recruiters and search firms, but I want to dig even deeper for you so that you can make an informed decision. At the end of the day, if I can help you make a great Number 2 hire, whether you consider working with VisionSpark or not, then I will feel good about helping you get what you need to succeed at a higher, Visionary level.

As an entrepreneur, I am passionate about helping other entrepreneurs because I understand that innovation and creativity are what drive our society and make the world a better place. I passionately believe that we need more entrepreneurs and that entrepreneurs are often misunderstood and underestimated. Yes, it would be wonderful if after reading this book you gave me a call to have a conversation about how we may help you, but I want to give you the best perspectives and insights I can offer so that you make the decisions that are best for you.

As you already see, my perspective is that 99 percent of the time, it is the best choice for an entrepreneurial company to use a search firm when hiring a Number 2 Leader. I have given you many rationales for this perspective, so I will assume that you are tracking with me on this. The next step, and this chapter's purpose, is to put you in the pilot's seat when interviewing potential search firms.

The Power of Questions

If you remember the sample question I shared with you from our candidate research interview process—the one about the candidate's greatest accomplishment—then you will see the power of the right question. We could spend days discussing how and why questions work the way they do, but let's stick to a couple of basics to start with.

Perhaps the most important thing to understand is that questions open a kind of vacuum that needs to be filled. When a question is asked, it begs an answer. As an entrepreneur, you already know this instinctively. Asking questions is what got you where you are today.

In that sample question from our candidate search interview, we already know the right answer, and at this point you already have enough knowledge to ask some of those sorts of questions.

But rather than asking yes or no questions, such as, "Is your fee a percentage of the position's salary?" you should ask: "Can you please explain your fee structure?" These more open-ended questions create a larger vacuum that will give you more information, including things you cannot predict.

It is also useful to ask questions that redirect the conversation. For example, you have just received the right answer to a question you asked, and you would like to move on to something else. An effective way to do this is to say something like: "We haven't yet talked about how you are going to get to know me and our culture. Can you explain how you would do that?" The point is that as the interviewer, you want to guide the conversation into the areas that matter most to you. If you find that the tables have turned and that you are being asked more questions than you are asking, it's time to change directions and guide the conversation back to what you need to know. Let's go over what some of those topics should be.

Important Questions to Ask

The first question you probably want to ask is: How much is this going to cost? Perhaps the best way to ask this question is to ask if they could tell you about their fee structure. What you will find is that there are three structures: percentage of salary, hourly rate, and a flat fee. The most common is the percentage of salary, and those range between 20 percent to 35 percent of salary.

There's the hourly rate model as well. If they have an hourly approach, you need to find out when the meter will be running and how time will be tallied. You also must watch what motivates them to close a deal and find someone. We recently took on a new client who had already spent $120,000 with an hourly rate search firm. This search firm was not successful in finding a strong candidate and the client had nothing to show for it except a six-figure expense.

No matter what fee structure the firm uses, you must know in advance what is included and what the rules are. For example, if you have two candidates for the role and one salary would be higher than the other, would a higher fee be charged if you go with the lower salary candidate? The devil is in the details, as they say.

You should also ask if they are open to external interviews or third-party specialists. Some firms will be against this and will not want further analysis of a candidate because they are concerned that you will drop the candidate and they will not get their fee. Others may have no problem with that because they get how important it is for you to find the right person.

It's also wise to ask the firm how they plan to get to know you, your needs, and your company's culture so that you find someone who will work well with you. What methods will they use? How much time will they allocate to this? Along those same lines, you should ask them the details about their evaluation process. Are they evaluating just from resumes, or are they focusing on leadership qualities, behaviors, traits, and values?

You will also want to know about their success rate and placement rate. Placement rate is a metric that tells you the odds that they will find somebody for you. Success rate, on the other hand, refers to how long their placements stay in the position. How many people are still there after one year? Eighteen months? Two years?

And for your specific purpose, you should ask what percentage of their business is focused on hiring the Number 2 Leader. On a related note, you will want to know what their experience is in hiring leaders, like successfully placing a COO for an entrepreneurial company. How many searches have you done? Can you give me references for successful Number 2s that you have placed?

Of course, you also need to be clear about *when they will consider the job done.*

Do they have an onboarding process? What is it, and how does it work? What level employee will be working on your search? How much experience do they have? Is there a dedicated person assigned to your search? And how long will the search process take? You should also ask how many projects they take on at once.

These questions will go a long way toward choosing the best search firm for you.

Next up, we need to talk about the biggest mistakes people make in hiring a Number 2 Leader.

66

THE GREATEST LEADER IS
NOT NECESSARILY THE ONE
WHO DOES THE GREATEST
THINGS. HE IS THE ONE THAT
GETS THE PEOPLE TO DO THE
GREATEST THINGS.

———————————

Ronald Reagan

CHAPTER SEVEN

The Biggest Mistakes in Hiring a Number 2 Leader (and How You Can Avoid Them)

We have already covered the huge costs involved—in time, money, and opportunity cost—when you hire the wrong Number 2 Leader, so let's go over the top mistakes that entrepreneurs make when hiring their Number 2. This will also help us put into perspective how things routinely go wrong in the hiring process, which is mostly a matter of trusting instinct and convention over science and process.

The most common mistake made in hiring your Number 2 is to give weight in your assessment of a candidate to the resume. Think about it. There is an industry devoted to writing resumes, so the chances that your candidate wrote their own are low. That already tells us that the resume is not a true representation of the candidate. And let's not forget either that 48 percent of resumes have outright lies in them, and virtually all of them have some form of embellishment. The resume is written, remember, to impress, not to give an exact portrayal of a candidate's mental acuity, character, business knowledge or strategic thinking capabilities.

Yet the resume is such a standard prop in the hiring process that we experience frame blindness, which means that our perspective or frame blinds us from seeing the resume's limited value. The resume matters, of course, in that it gives us a broad overview of a candidate's employment history and education, but even these things matter much less than their communication skills, mindset, and fit in relation to the Visionary's strengths.

The next most common pitfall for entrepreneurs when they set out to hire their Number 2 is hiring from a pool of one. This means that we get so homed in on one candidate that we lose objectivity and fall in love with our projection of what we believe the candidate will be like. If when pressed to explain why we are so convinced about this candidate, we say that it's a gut feeling or intuition, then it's time to be wary. You may be right, but you really need to accept that you may be wrong. Thorough assessments are needed, such as the Talent Impact Profile™.

A related mistake is to hire someone already on your team that you trust. This is not uncommon, as leaders we would rather hire the "devil we know" rather than "the devil we don't know." If you choose to consider a candidate for the Number 2 leader role that is currently on your team or someone you know well, then be sure to have them evaluated by a third party. At VisionSpark, this is a service we offer. Here are some scenarios that may occur: You have an amazing candidate and because of the evaluation, you are confident in their future and double down on your commitment to them. You will also know their strengths and any opportunities for development. Another possibility is that you find that this candidate falls short of the benchmark of a Number 2 leader, and you don't hire them. You then will have only invested a little time and money and saving you from hiring mistake that will have cost you well over six digits! The last scenario is that if they are not a great candidate and you hire them any way, you will see the accuracy of the evaluation. We have heard responses from our clients such as "Every concern you had about this candidate was spot on. I should have taken your advice and learned the hard way."

Lack of Role Clarity

The remaining big mistakes fit under the two categories of lack of role clarity and lack of effective hiring process.

In fact, if we had to name the two areas that must be in place for a good hire, these are those categories. Without knowing exactly what you need and are looking for, and without having a rigorous process to guarantee that you are getting what you want, you are just spinning the roulette wheel. But luck, as they say, is not a strategy.

Let's begin with role clarity.

Most mistakes involving lack of role clarity happen because you do not have a clear enough picture of how you will function optimally. Most entrepreneurs do not correctly see the value of their time, as we have discussed, and this means that they have not named their revenue-generating activities. Once you know what you should be focused on doing, then you can begin to have clarity about the Number 2 role. As I have pointed out several times already, you need to prioritize fit with the Visionary—which means you need to understand what the Visionary is bringing and what qualities and capabilities will be complementary.

Unfortunately, I have seen plenty of cases where there is this magical belief that you can just put someone in the position, and they will figure things out. I've seen people hire someone they golf with or play softball with because they have managerial experience and are looking for a job. Again, one of the most important hires you will ever make is being decided on a gut feeling or circumstances. As you know, I have personal experience hiring someone on gut instincts and completely disregarding the data. Things do not go well when that happens. In my case, I was fortunate that it was not a C-level hire and that things were quickly rectified.

Your Hiring Process

So how do you protect yourself and your business from making such mistakes? Your hiring process needs to be well thought out. As mentioned previously, you should set aside approximately 200 hours for the process. We have created a five-stage process that covers all the important steps and assessments. You must be intentional and committed to the search process, because hiring a Number 2 Leader who you can trust and trusts you is vital to your success and your business's success.

Stage 1: Role Clarity

The first stage of the hiring process is all about clarifying the role, getting buy-in from the team stakeholders, and clearly defining the fit for the Visionary. In our process, we refer to this stage as the Position Maximizer™ because it is where we establish maximum clarity of the position. This is an all-hands stage where you get real about what is essential and how the Number 2 will be involved with all key team members. You need to get buy-in from your stakeholders, and this is where that begins.

Stage 2: Posting & Screening

In this stage you will take what you have learned in the first stage and post your position profile. We call this stage Source and Screen because this is when you find candidates and do the first screening based on what you have identified as the assets you are looking for in a candidate. The goal here is to narrow your candidate pool to the top candidates. If you do not have enough candidates, you will need to revisit your position profile or find a deeper source of potential candidates to post to.

Stage 3: Calls with Top Candidates

In our system, we call this step or stage Culture Fit because we are focused on making calls with top candidates to determine their fit for the culture, especially with the Visionary. You may remember from earlier that we have specific qualities and capabilities we have determined to be essential, such as strategic thinking, people management, effective communication skills, team building, and time management (especially protecting the Visionary's time).

Stage 4: Assessment & Deep Interviews

This stage is all about leadership assessment, which we call the Right Fit Profiler™. This is where we assess the remaining candidates for their mental acuity, communication skills, business knowledge, and more. We use science-based assessments that give us what we need to figure out if a candidate is the right fit.

Stage 5: Final Interview

You will know the quality of your process by the quality of candidates who make it to this final stage, which we call Final Interview and Offer. This is an exciting stage of the process, and the energy is high. Keeping your perspective on finding the thunder for your Visionary's lightning is essential here.

When your hiring process is effective and efficient, you will take care of all the issues that can derail your hiring process. Another advantage of hiring a search firm to handle the process for you is that experts from the outside will have a much easier time noticing organizational and cultural issues that are simmering below the surface. Sorting these issues out is another bonus of an effective hiring process.

As a final note, I should mention that not all companies will benefit from hiring a Number 2. If you are not serious about growth, then this will be too much of a commitment for you. But for those entrepreneurs who want more freedom and more growth for their business, hiring your Number 2 Leader is the way to go.

66

TO ANY ENTREPRENEUR: IF YOU WANT TO DO IT, DO IT NOW. IF YOU DON'T, YOU'RE GOING TO REGRET IT.

———————

Catherine Cook

Bonus Chapter - Your Other Critical Hire: The Value in Hiring an Outside Business Coach

For this bonus chapter, I'd like for us to imagine that you have hired your Number 2. Time to roll up the sleeves and get to work, right? You have gotten clear on what will be involved in taking your company to the next level, and you have hired your Number 2 Leader, so let's take this show on the road!

While the excitement is called for, I want to point out that there is an incredible opportunity here for you to make a wise investment in hiring an outside consultant to help you implement and guide you through what will most likely be deep changes to your organization and operations.

The timing is perfect for you to bring in an outside consultant who specializes in such work and understands entrepreneurial cultures and all the challenges and opportunities that go with companies like yours. We have seen incredible results when the hiring of a Number 2 Leader is paired with working with an outside consultant, specifically with what is now often called an Implementer, business coach, guide, or facilitator. You can also think of them as an executor—someone who specializes in making sure that your new systems are properly implemented.

The Coach's Role

First, let me reassure you that you are not hiring another employee. A business coach will meet with your leadership team probably once a quarter and then annually for maybe five days per year over two years or so. Costs for such a consultant vary of course on their experience and your industry, but what they offer in terms of your success with your new Number 2 Leader is priceless.

Let me explain. You need to put your plan into action, and the more effectively and efficiently you do this, the faster you will reap the benefits of your plan. It is most likely also true that even though you have a plan, you probably do not know how you are going to make it all work. In fact, it is quite likely that the deeper you dig in the name of improvement, the more you will come face to face with systemic limitations and previously unknown issues that need to be dealt with. You may even realize that you do not have all the right people in the right seats to do everything you need to do. This is where having an expert in your corner, someone who has traveled this road and knows where to look and what questions to ask, could be the difference between meeting your quarterly goals and a slow transitional meltdown.

This business coach, however, is not there to tell you what to do. They help you decide what needs to be done and then make sure it gets done. They are part leadership coach and part facilitator, someone who can understand your KPIs from the perspective of your strategy and someone who can read the room when things are not working out. Specifically, they help you develop your ninety-day goals and then help keep the team on track in your quarterly meetings. We see that companies who have outside help are much more successful at meeting their short and long-term goals. As an outside expert, they are typically better able to sniff out trouble spots than anyone from within, including turf issues. They might say, for example, "It seems like your salesperson wants to grow and your ops leader is resistant. What's going on here?" This kind of input is gold.

Hiring an outside consultant after hiring your Number 2 Leader also sends a message to the team and to your Number 2 Leader that you are going all in on taking the business to new heights. You are providing real support to your Number 2 Leader for building and implementing new systems and organizational practices while also getting expert guidance from someone who specializes in coaching entrepreneurial companies through such a growth plan.

The Value of Hiring a Business Coach

Your coach has the responsibility to prioritize and oversee the implementation of your business strategy and new vision. This includes using proven tools and processes to steer leadership teams into healthy unity around the entrepreneur's vision, ensuring that everyone is rowing in the same direction. They bring valuable perspective to the table, as they have worked with many companies in a variety of industries.

In a time of change, there will be resistance. Having a trusted outside advisor coupled with your new Number 2 Leader will ensure that you continue to build momentum and the confidence of your team and their reports.

This capable business coach knows that the clock is ticking on getting results that provide a shared sense of unity and purpose. This is one of the main reasons why we recommend hiring a coach after hiring your Number 2 Leader (by the way, coaching is not something that we provide at VisionSpark, but we will be happy to refer you to a qualified coach if you contact us). We have seen repeatedly how taking this added step amplifies productivity and keeps the team on track during those first two years after hiring a Number 2 Leader.

Perhaps the superpower of a coach is to see the forest for the trees: they identify themes across your issues list and implement tools to eliminate them and reduce friction.

It's one thing to **want** to become a company that always learns from every project and builds company knowledge and another to accomplish that goal.

A business coach's experience in navigating the waters you are in as you grow your company through hiring a Number 2 Leader will guarantee efficient use of your time and resources at a time when getting good numbers up on the board is mission critical. In short, the value in hiring an outside consultant, a trusted business coach, for this stage in your company's growth comes down to the reasons why you hired your Number 2; you need to focus on what you do best while getting the best possible help for everything else.

66

THE ONLY WAY TO DO GREAT WORK IS TO LOVE WHAT YOU DO.

———————————

Steve Jobs

Conclusion

C ongratulations, we've reached the end of the book, but this isn't an ending, it's the beginning of your company's much bigger, brighter future.

Which direction will you take your business in? Are you ready to find your Number 2 Leader?

If you are ready, then I invite you to take the next step by scheduling a Discovery Call with a Client Strategist at VisionSpark. We'll ask you questions about your business and walk you through our process step-by-step. That way you'll have specific answers about the search process for your business and can decide whether it's right for you. Just visit our website or book an appointment in our calendar VisionSparkSearch.com/2-Leader

Thanks for allowing me to be a part of your journey.

I wish you every success!

About the Author

Alec Broadfoot is the Visionary and Founder of VisionSpark—a premium search firm helping fast-growing companies make critical decisions by hiring the right people in the right seats, every time. For more than a decade VisionSpark has helped hundreds of entrepreneurial companies hire key leaders. With the highest placement rate in the industry, VisionSpark is recognized in the Inc. 5000™ Regionals as one of the fastest-growing companies in the Midwest.

Alec is a frequent speaker at Vistage International, Conference for Companies running on EOS®, Entrepreneurs' Organization, J.P Morgan Chase®, and various podcasts and webinars with organizations like Strategic Coach®.

Alec lives in Ohio with his family.

CONNECT WITH ALEC

Follow him on your favorite social media platforms today.

VisionSparkSearch.com/2-Leader

Praise for VisionSpark

Entrepreneurs who need a "Who" to elevate their leadership teams, look no further. Alec and his team at VisionSpark use science-based tools (which I've personally found very insightful) and a proven process to help you recruit exactly who you're looking for, especially when it comes to hiring your Number 2 Leader.

Shannon Waller,
Entrepreneurial Team Strategist, Strategic Coach ®

VisionSpark took the burden off of me. Instead of trying to do everything myself, they provided expert guidance and support throughout the entire hiring process. They helped me define the role based on my company's values and needs. Attempting to do it alone can be overwhelming and time- consuming, and it's difficult to know if you're making the right decisions. With VisionSpark's help, I was able to find a leader who not only had the necessary skills but also fit in with our company culture.

Ryan Flynn,
Founder & CEO, Charmac

Before I hired Larissa, I felt like I had so much on my plate that was slowing me down. As an entrepreneur, I knew that I needed someone who could help me operate in my "zone of genius." Larissa is the missing puzzle piece that I was looking for—she understands my business goals and shares my passion for growth. Working with VisionSpark has been a wonderful experience—they found me a Number 2 that I can trust. Larissa is now taking point on several other leadership openings that VisionSpark is helping us find! This has helped me save time and focus on what I do best.

Katrina Ubell, MD,
Master Certified Life and Weight Loss Coach,
Weight Loss for Busy Physicians

Before we hired our Number 2 Leader, our leadership team was strong but lacked the structure that a COO would bring. After seeing Alec present, I knew that we needed to hire an Integrator to help take us to the next level. VisionSpark's commitment to finding the right person for the job by focusing on cultural fit, rather than just the most experienced or expensive candidate, was an appealing part of their process. By following their process, we were able to open ourselves up to opportunities that we may have missed otherwise; their expertise resulted in finding the right candidate for our organization.

Erik Piasio,
President, American Surgical Company

Before I hired my Number 2 Leader, life was painful. Now I have a dedicated Integrator/COO and my life is so much better! Don't hesitate to hire your Number 2 Leader, just do it. You can do it yourself if you have the time but it's hard to know what you're getting or who is the right person for you. I used the experts: VisionSpark. It takes the time off of you. If you're like most Visionaries, there's just not enough time. I really liked the discovery phase and how they outlined what we needed in an Integrator. My search consultant and I met weekly to keep me informed. It was an excellent process. It's nice knowing what to expect. I learned a lot and know what I could do differently as we continue to search for more compatible leaders.

Kimberly E Wright MD
FACOG, Owner/Visionary, The Wright Center for Women's
Health

From the perspective of a candidate for a leadership role, I thought they did an excellent job. They were very thorough, and their screening tests and the questions were on point with what you were looking for in a new employee. Each step was relevant, which is quite the opposite of most hiring processes which can be predictable and disingenuous. Five stars from me!

Jenny Lusher, Integrator, Midwest Aerial

Alec and the VisionSpark team are the best at finding your right fit Number 2 Leader. They understand their clients' unique needs and always go above and beyond to deliver exceptional service. I highly recommend them for finding top- notch talent and expertise!

Chad Johnson,
Entrepreneur, Author, Coach, Father of Eleven

Before hiring my Number 2 Leader, I was trying to re-grow the company from an earlier bad hire. I had done a decent job but realized it wasn't my best skill. I wanted to scale the business, but my skill was more of the big picture Visionary. Working with VisionSpark enabled me to delegate the challenging task of hiring the right person to their knowledgeable team that did all the heavy lifting and kept me involved and informed every step of the way. VisionSpark conducted a thorough and comprehensive hiring process up to the very last day, as the very last candidate that came in ended up being the best fit for Lawyers with Purpose! Now two years later she has become the Number One in scaling my vision!

David J. Zumpano, CPA, Esq.,
Founder, Lawyers with Purpose, LLC

THIS BOOK IS PROTECTED INTELLECTUAL PROPERTY

EASY IP™

The author of this book values Intellectual Property. The book you just read is protected by Easy IP™, a proprietary process, which integrates blockchain technology giving Intellectual Property "Global Protection." By creating a "Time-Stamped" smart contract that can never be tampered with or changed, we establish "First Use" that tracks back to the author.

Easy IP™ functions much like a Pre-Patent™ since it provides an immutable "First Use" of the Intellectual Property. This is achieved through our proprietary process of leveraging blockchain technology and smart contracts. As a result, proving "First Use" is simple through a global and verifiable smart contract. By protecting intellectual property with blockchain technology and smart contracts, we establish a "First to File" event.

Powered By Easy IP™

LEARN MORE AT EASYIP.TODAY